# 101 MIND BENDING GEOGRAPHY

## FUN FACTS

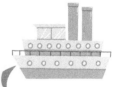

**IS THE SAHARA DESERT REALLY THE LARGEST DESERT?**

**WHAT IS THE DIFFERENCE BETWEEN A JUNGLE AND A RAINFOREST?**

Sources used throughout this book are verified using Wikipedia®, unless explicitly stated along with the fact. Most facts stated within this book expose or reiterate common misconceptions about our world, point out technicalities that are generally overlooked and reveal just straight-up unusual facts.

# B.C. Lester Books

### Geography publications for the people since 2019.

**Visit us at www.bclesterbooks.com for more!**

As keen geography enthusiasts, this book was created as a compilation of unusual geography facts that wowed us the most over the years.

**We dedicate this book to all us curious people.**

# A QUICK MESSAGE FOR US...

## THANKS FOR PURCHASING THIS BOOK...

...we really hope you enjoy it. If you have the chance, then all feedback on Amazon is greatly appreciated. We have put a lot of effort into making this book, so if you are not completely satisfied, please email us at ben@bclesterbooks.com and we will do our best to address any issues. If you have any suggestions, want to get in touch or want to send us your score, then email at the same address - ben@bclesterbooks.com

## IS THIS BOOK MISPRINTED?

Printing presses, like humans, aren't quite perfect. Send us an email at ben@bclesterbooks.com with a photo of the misprint, and we will get another copy sent out to you!

## WHO ARE WE AT B.C. LESTER BOOKS?

B.C. Lester Books is a small publishing firm of three people based in Buckinghamshire, UK. We aim to provide quality works in all things geography, for kids and adults, with varying interests. We have already released a selection of activity, trivia and fact books and are working hard to bring you wider selection. Have a suggestion for us? Then email ben@bclesterbooks.com. We are all ears!

## HAVE EVEN MORE QUIZZING FUN WITH OUR GIFT TO YOU: A 3-IN-1 GEOGRAPHY QUIZ BOOK!

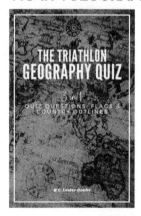 

### Go here to grab your FREE copy!
www.bclesterbooks.com/freebies/

## CONTENTS

# 1. THE FULL NAME OF THAILAND'S CAPITAL, BANGKOK, HAS 168 LETTERS!

The full name of the city is Krung Thep Mahanakhon Amon Rattanakosin Mahinthara Yuthaya Mahadilok Phop Noppharat Ratchathani Burirom Udomratchaniwet Mahasathan Amon Piman Awatan Sathit Sakkathattiya Witsanukam Prasit. This translates to: City of angels, great city of immortals, magnificent city of the nine gems, seat of the king, city of royal palaces, home of gods incarnate, erected by Vishvakarman at Indra's behest. As this was a bit of a mouthful for the locals, the Thai name is often stated as Krung Thep Maha Nakhon, or even more simply as Krung Thep. This indeed is the longest town name in the world.

# 2. SOME BUILDINGS AND SKYSCRAPERS IN NEW YORK CITY ARE SO BIG, THEY HAVE THEIR OWN ZIP CODE (POSTCODE)!

Yep, thats right! To be exact, 42 buildings have the privilege of owning their own zip code! Buildings that have qualified include the Empire State Building, MetLife Building and Chrysler Building. The main determinant for having their own zip code, however, does not lie in the buildings size, rather the volume of mail. For example, the One World Trade Center does not have its own zip code, but the Empire State, with over 150 businesses addressed there, has enough mail to be given its own zip.

## 3. SEA WATER HAS AROUND 20,000,000 TONS OF GOLD DISSOLVED IN IT.

Yes you heard right. The price of Gold is always changing, but estimates say that is is around $700 trillion worth, or roughly 10 times the world gross domestic product. This gold are particles dissolved in the water, just like sodium and chloride (salt) and can be extracted by simply evaporating the water! The problem is that the concentration of gold in seawater is so dilute that attempts to cash in on 'mining' this gold has always been unprofitable. For perspective, to find just 1 ounce (28.5 grams) of gold, you would need around 2 billion (2,000,000,000) tons of seawater...

## 4. THE MOST REMOTE PLACE IN THE WORLD IS POINT NEMO.

It is the furthest point on Earth's surface from land and technically described as the oceanic pole of inaccessibility'. Although it has a longer name, the popularized name is Point Nemo from the latin word meaning 'no-one'. The nearest landmass is over 1000 miles (1609km) away, but if you are looking for an inhabited landmass, this figure is nearer 1600 miles (2575km). This means that the closest humans to Point Nemo for some time are astronauts flying in the International Space Station!

## 5. THE UNITED KINGDOM IS LARGER THAN CANADA AND AUSTRALIA COMBINED.

Just to clarify, when we say larger, we are talking population here! Words don't do this statistic justice, so here are a few numbers. The UK's 66 million people is 2 million more than the combination of Canada's 38 million and Australia's 26 million! On the contrary, the combined land surface area of Canada and Australia is over **72** times the land surface area of the United Kingdom. If this isn't enough, exists is an even more extreme comparison, Indonesia's island of Java is just over half the size of the UK and has a population of 144 million. This is also roughly the population of Russia, whose land area is over **200** times larger!

## 6. AYER'S ROCK / ULURU MAY BE BIGGER THAN YOU THINK!

You will at some point see one of Australia's great attractions across the internet, and see a big red rock. Often though, these pictures don't capture how enormous this rock really is! The rock formation protrudes 348m (1142ft) from the ground and the total length of the rock is 2.2 miles long, or around the same length as around 33 football pitches!

## 7. MOUNT EVEREST, THE TALLEST MOUNTAIN, CAN FIT IN THE DEEPEST PART OF THE OCEAN.

The deepest part of the ocean is known as Challenger Deep in the Mariana trench, part of the Pacific Ocean. The maximum known depth here is a massive 10,984 metres (36,037ft) dwarfing Mt Everest's 8848 metres (29,029ft) tall.

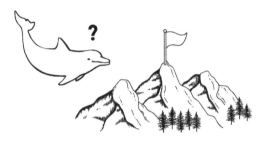

## 8. IN THE DEAD SEA, IT'S NEARLY IMPOSSIBLE TO DROWN.

Normally, you can float in water to a certain extent, treading water and for short periods of time; by laying on your back, but not in the Dead Sea! People have laid back in the ocean and read their favorite book in this sea, thanks to the saltiness of the water. Because it is 8 to 9 times saltier than average sea water, the Dead Sea is alot more dense; meaning the less dense humans (consisting of around 70% water) will lay on the surface when lying back flat.

## 9. FOR SOME OF THE YEAR, YOU CAN WALK FROM THE USA TO RUSSIA.

This may sound inconceivable without a boat, but there is a place between Russia and the U.S. state of Alaska, where the 2 countries are separated by a 2.5 mile (4.0km) strait. These places are islands called Big Diomede, located on the Russian side and Little Diomede, located on the American side, and sit roughly in the middle between the Russian and American mainland. In the winter and spring, the temperature is low enough for the seawater to freeze over and to allow the citizens to cross the border by foot. If you are more of a swimmer, then this is also possible, the route being completed in 1987 by Lynne Cox during the Cold War.

## 10. THERE ARE SEVERAL SETTLEMENTS WITH THE WORLD'S SHORTEST NAME.

So you have heard of the world's longest city name at a huge 168 letters, but what about the other extreme? Can you think of any place with 2 letters, or even 3 letters? Neither can we, let alone 1 letter! There are several settlements in Norway and Sweden with one letter, a large proportion thanks to being named river and island, which in the Scandinavian languages is Å and Ö respectively... Other settlements with 1 letter include the French village of Y.

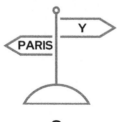

# 11. THE WORLD'S LARGEST WAR MEMORIAL IS A ROAD IN AUSTRALIA.

At the end of World War One, many returning soldiers in Australia were offered jobs building what was to become one of Australia's great attractions. By the time of the completion of the road, named the Great Ocean Road, in 1932, the road spanned 150 miles. The road was soon dedicated to the lives lost during the First World War, making it the world's largest war memorial.

# 12. THERE IS AN ISLAND, WITHIN A LAKE, WITHIN AN ISLAND, WITHIN A LAKE, WITHIN AN ISLAND.

Feel free to read this all again, we did. Vulcan Point is an island, located in Main Crater Lake, located on Volcano island, located in Lake Taal, located on Luzon island in the Philippines. Since the volcanoes eruption in 2020, the Main Crater lake appears to have evaporated. Fear not, here are other examples of this in Canada and Indonesia, all of which follow the same recursive pattern but start with much smaller(and nameless) islands.

# 13. ICELAND IS GROWING BY 2 INCHES (5CM) A YEAR.

Iceland straddles the border between the North American and Eurasian tectonic plate. As these tectonic plates are both oceanic and are moving apart, a divergent boundary, this creates new land. Most of this new land forms the Atlantic sea bed, but in Icelands case, creates new land and gives the island large amount of geothermal activity, seen above land in the form of thermal baths, geysers and volcanoes.

# 14. THE PACIFIC OCEAN IS SHRINKING BY AROUND 1 INCH (2.5CM) A YEAR.

Yes, this follows the reasoning of the previous fun fact! The North American and Eurasian plate in their Atlantic boundary is creating land at the expense of land at their Pacific boundary. These tectonic plates in the Pacific are responsible for the height of the Andes and Rockies mountain ranges, the infamous San Andreas fault, and the ring of fire, a pattern of active volcanoes roughly following the plate boundaries.

## 15. THERE'S A TOWN IN THE U.S.A. WITH A POPULATION OF ONE.

Monowi, Nebraska is a settlement with a woman named Elsie Eiler as the sole resident. The settlement peaked in size, hitting around 150 in the 1930s, but has since declined, with much of the younger population finding better opportunities in the larger cities. For a few years, Monowi had a population of 2 until the death of Eiler's husband. Eiler is the town mayor, therefore granting herself a liquor license and paying taxes to herself. She also runs a tavern called the Monowi Tavern that caters for passer-bys.

## 16. IT'S STILL DECEMBER 30TH IN SOME PLACES WHEN THE FIRST COUNTRY CELEBRATES NEW YEARS.

While it's well known that certain countries celebrate New Years before other countries, to what extent does this occur? It's maybe more than you think, as when the first place hits midnight on January 1st, in the last place, the time and date is 10pm on December 30th! The first country is Kiribati, a Pacific island nation in the unusual UTC+14:00 time zone, and the last place are uninhabited islands belonging to the U.S., in the UTC-12:00 time zone. UTC-11:00, sitting at 11pm on December 30th during Kiribati's New Years, includes the inhabited islands of Niue, American Samoa and more.

## 17. EARTH'S COLDEST SPOT IS COLD ENOUGH TO FREEZE CARBON DIOXIDE.

Earth's coldest recorded temperature occured in Russia's Vostok station on Antarctica in 1983. They recorded a chilly -128.6°F (-89.2°C), a temperature cold enough to turn carbon dioxide into it's solid form, dry ice! Carbon dioxide freezes at -109.2°F (-78.5°C), a temperature which the Vostok Station records several times a year. However, in practice, the Carbon Dioxide in air does not freeze until even lower temperatures because air is a mixture of gases, but if you had a container of pure carbon dioxide and left it outside, it may very well freeze!

## 18. ROCKS CAN WALK IN DEATH VALLEY, CALIFORNIA.

Rocks appear to have been walking in the lakebeds around Death Valley, with some weighing more than the average human, leaving a trail across the landscape. In the Racetrack Playa, ice encrusted rocks, meltwater, and a perfect storm, knock rocks off the surrounding mountains, and the ice allows the rock to slide across the flat landscape for miles, leaving behind a trail that gives the impression that they are searching for greener pastures.

# 19. A MORNING IN PARTS OF RUSSIA IS AN EVENING IN OTHER PARTS.

Russia, the world's largest country, spans an astonishing 11 time zones! As people are getting ready to go to work in Western Russia, in places such as St. Petersburg and Moscow, people may be enjoying their dinner in East Russia, in places such as Vladivostok.

# 20. THE SAHARA DESERT WILL BECOME GRASSLAND IN 15,000 YEARS.

The Sahara Desert is largely a sandy, hot, inhospitable area but it won't always be like this. In fact, it was also not always like this. The Sahara Desert follows a 20,000 year cycle between arid desert and grassland with vegetation and lakes, caused by the change in orientation of the Earth's axis as it rotates around the sun! Evidence suggests that until around 5000BC, the Sahara was also highly vegetated.

## 21. THE SMALLEST COUNTRY IN THE WORLD IS AN EIGHTH OF THE SIZE OF CENTRAL PARK IN NEW YORK.

The smallest country in the world is probably smaller than you thought! Vatican City, located in Rome, Italy, is a fully independent nation with around 800 people living inside. It's size is 0.19 sq miles (0.49 sq km). The country is ruled by the Pope, and created in 1929 to settle tensions between the Holy See and Italy.  Today, the impressive St. Peters Basilica draws millions of tourists every year.

## 22. YELLOWSTONE NATIONAL PARK IS HOME TO AN ACTIVE "SUPERVOLCANO".

Yellowstone National Park in Wyoming is a popular destination for tourists, offering a range of natural attractions such as waterfalls, wildlife, canyons and the famous Old Faithful geyser. Beneath all this is a "supervolcano", a volcano that has deposited over 240 cubic miles (1000 cubic km) in an eruption. In other words, should the volcano erupt, it would likely devastate the whole state. The volcano is active, having erupted 3 times in the past, but fortunately for the visitors of Yellowstone, it's last eruption was over 500,000 years ago. Phew!

## 23. ISTANBUL IS THE LARGEST CITY LOCATED IN 2 DIFFERENT CONTINENTS.

Istanbul, Turkey spans a long history, being the capital of the Roman Empire, Latin Empire and Ottoman Empire, under the names Constantinople and Byzantium. It's strategic location as the gateway of Europe, and subsequently along the Silk Road, meant that many nations throughout history fought for it's control. The city straddles the Bosphorus Strait, the official border between Europe and Asia. The historic and commercial centre lies on the European side, along with 2 thirds of the population of the city. Therefore, Istanbul is the largest city in Europe and one of the largest in the world.

## 24. ALASKA IS THE USA'S WESTERNMOST AND EASTERNMOST STATE.

A simple look on the map makes it's westernmost claim obvious but its easternmost claim looks a little more cryptic. The Western and Eastern hemispheres meet at 180 longitude, also known as the antimeridian. This antimeridian is therefore the easternmost point of the Eastern hemisphere, and westernmost of the West hemisphere. The Aleutian Islands in Alaska extend Southwest from mainland Alaska and pass the antimeridian, formally entering into the Eastern hemisphere and therefore by definition, makes them the easternmost part of the USA.

## 25. SPAIN IS BOTH A EUROPEAN AND AFRICAN COUNTRY.

If you associated Spain with Europe, then you would be correct. However, 3 of it's autonomous communities (somewhat like states/counties/provinces) are located in Africa! The largest one is the Canary Islands, a group of islands west of Morocco that is geographically Africa, but politically in Europe, being fully integrated in the European Union. The other 2 is Ceuta and Mellila, small autonomous Spanish exclaves on the African mainland, making Spain the only European country to exert sovereignty over lsnf in mainland Africa.

## 26. MEXICO CITY IS SINKING NEARLY A YARD/METRE A YEAR.

Mexico City was originally an Aztec City, built in the 1300s by filling the Lago de Texcoco to create an artificial island. The Spanish further developed the city, and due to the locals reliance of the aquifer beneath the city for drinking water, the city sinks around 3 feet (90cm) a year. In 60 years, Mexico City has sunk 32 feet (9.8m)!

## 27. THE TOTAL SURFACE AREA OF CANADA'S LAKES IS LARGER THAN TEXAS.

Texas is a rather large state in it's own right. It is larger than any country solely in Europe, and USA's second largest state after Alaska. But when it comes to tallying up Canada's 2,000,000 freshwater lakes, the total surface area completely dwarfs Texas. Infact, around 9% of Canada's total area is freshwater lake, meaning that they take up around 350,000 sq miles (900,000 sq km). Of the 2,000,000 lakes, 563 are larger than 39 sq miles (100 sq km).

## 28. INDONESIA HAS THE WORLD'S LARGEST ISLAM POPULATION.

When it comes to Islam, you may think to the Middle East to find the largest population. Whilst a large proportion do live there, Indonesia in South East Asia takes the crown for the largest Islam following, down to its huge population. The most populous middle eastern country is Egypt, with a population of 100,000,000, whilst Indonesia is over 270,000,000, just behind the USA's population. Around 87% of Indonesia adhere to Islam, which isn't the highest percentage (Egypt is around 90%), but is still enough to put Indonesia in the lead. The 2nd, 3rd and 4th largest Islam populations belong to Pakistan, India and Bangladesh respectively, and interestingly enough, none of those countries are in the Middle East.

## 29. THE LARGEST DESERT IN THE WORLD IS NOT THE SAHARA DESERT.

The Sahara Desert is enormous, being able to fit contiguous USA within it's boundaries, but there is an even larger desert that has disguised itself, as it is made mostly of water. This desert is Antarctica, and is roughly 1.5 times larger than the Sahara. You may associate deserts with hot, sandy places, but a desert, by definition, is generally an area which receives less than 250mm (10 inches) of rainfall yearly (although geographers may consider additional factors to further distinguish a desert). Antarctica, with the majority of its land recording rainfall below this threshold amount, qualifies for being a desert, although to make a distinction with typical hot deserts, it is called a polar desert.

## 30. THESE 2 NEIGHBOURING ISLANDS ARE 21 HOURS APART.

Situated just 2.5 miles (4km) apart, the Diomede Islands between Russia and the United States have such a big difference in time because the International Date Line (IDL) crosses right in the middle of them. Big Diomede, the russian Diomede is in the UTC+12:00 time zone, whereas the American Little Diomede follows UTC-9:00. This little caveat earned the 2 islands the nicknames the Tomorrow Island (Big Diomede) and the Yesterday Island (Little Diomede).

## 31. WITH 56 CHARACTERS, THIS COUNTRY HAS THE LONGEST OFFICIAL NAME.

The country's official name in most cases outlines the political or governmental structure of the country. For example, Russian Federation, People's Republic of China, French Republic and so on. So it may be hard to estimate who would have the longest, but this record belongs to the United Kingdom - whose official name is the United Kingdom of Great Britain and Northern Ireland. Until 2013, Libya held the record with Al Jumahiriyah al Arabiyah al Libiyah ash Shabiyah al Ishtirakiyah al Uzma, totalling 63 characters. Since then, the official name is now the State of Libya.

## 32. PAPUA NEW GUINEA TAKES THE MEANING OF MULTILINGUAL TO ANOTHER LEVEL.

Papua New Guinea has the most most spoken languages in the world, with around 820 languages spoken by it's population. It's society, largely based on social clans and sustainable farming means that on average, each language has only around 7000 speakers, the largest of which is called Enga, with around 200,000 speakers. Furthermore, Papua New Guinea is one of the least explored nations in the world, with estimates suggesting that uncontacted tribes could very well increase the total count of languages.

## 33. LET IT SNOW... IN HAWAII.

With it's famous Waikiki Beach, great surfing waters, palm trees and tropical climate, the island chain is a popular destination across the world. However, drive to the top of the islands largest mountain, Mauna Kea, in the winter and you could make a snowman. Mauna Kea translates to 'White Mountain' because it is often snow capped.

## 34. THE INFAMOUS BERMUDA TRIANGLE IS NO MORE DANGEROUS THAN OTHER REGIONS OF THE SEA.

The Bermuda Triangle, a region of the sea equal to a triangle drawn from Bermuda, Florida and Puerto Rico, has been long associated with mysterious disappearings of ships and planes in the area, sometimes attributed to the paranormal or even extraterrestrial life. Claims of unusual differences began in the 50s, and gained notoriety in the 60s following more supposed disappearances. Because at the time, findings were not conclusive, alot of independent theories arose, from violent weather as explanantions, to UFOs and Atlantis City responsible for the outcome. Today, it is widely acknowledged that documented incidents in the Bermuda Triangle were false, exaggerated or later exacerbated by authors. United States coast guard confirm that ships do not sink at higher rates in this area, and the Lloyds Banking do not charge higher insurance premiums for ships crossing this area.

## 35. THE SHORTEST FLIGHT IN THE WORLD IS LESS THAN A MINUTE LONG.

The Orkney Islands in Scotland are a group of islands that can be found just north of Great Britain's northernmost point, John O'Groats. The group of 70 islands is well connected with various ferry's connecting the inhabited islands, as well as flights. The shortest scheduled flight in the world may be found here too, with 2 islands, Westray and Papa Westray, being connected by a 1.7 miles (2.7km) filght that in good weather can be done in under one minute! The record time for this journey is 47 seconds. This does not include the time on the runway so in practice, you would be in the plane a little longer than the claimed journey times.

## 36. THE WINTER IN THE HOTTEST PLACE ON EARTH IS WARMER THAN MIAMI AND LOS ANGELES IN THE SUMMER.

Dallol, Ethiopia hold the record for being the hottest average inhabited place in the world, with an average day in July reaching 45.6°C (114.1°F). In January, Dallol somewhat cools down, with average days reaching only 36.1°C (97°F). Compare this to downtown Los Angeles' July average high temperature of 28.4°C (84.1°F), and Miami's 32.7°C (90.9^F). Dallol's unusually warm climate may be attributed to it's location in a desert, over 100 metres below sea-level and it's proximity to the Equator and the hot Red Sea.

## 37. DO YOU LIKE SNOW? HERE'S THE BEST PLACE TO BE.

If you are a fan of snow, then you will love Aomori, Japan. Japan may not be the first place that comes to mind when you think of snow, but the country, by the amount of snowfall, is the snowiest country in the world. Aomori, on the northern shore of the island of Honshu, records some of the heaviest snowfall in the world. The average snowfall in a year here is 669cm (263 inches) and the record snow cover was recorded at 209cm (82 inches) in February 1945. For comparison, snowfall in Ottawa, one of the coldest capitals in the world, averages 175cm (69 inches) in a year. Japan's snowiness may be attributed to the cold, dry Siberian wind blowing over the Sea of Japan and picking up moisture there, similar to lake effect snow, seen in the Great Lakes region. However, unlike the Great Lakes, most of the Sea of Japan does not freeze in the winter.

## 38. FRANCE'S LONGEST BORDER IS WITH BRAZIL.

You heard right. To simply explain, France has 18 regions (somewhat like states/provinces/counties). One of the regions is French Guiana, located on the South American mainland. French Guiana shares a 450 mile (730km) border with Brazil, 42 miles (73km) longer than France's second longest border with Belgium. French Guiana to France may be compared to Alaska to the USA, it is part of the EU, the currency used is Euro and French is the most spoken language.

## 39. MIDDLE EASTERN COUNTRIES IMPORT THEIR SAND.

In many Middle Eastern countries, there has been a surge of construction as many have found their wealth through oil. Whilst many of the countries in question are surrounded by sand, unfortunately, this desert sand isn't very good for the construction of buildings, as it is so smooth from years of weathering. So budgets are set aside to import coarser sand from places such as Australia!

## 40. FRANCE IS THE WORLD'S FAVORITE VACATION SPOT.

In 2018, France welcomed nearly 90 million people from international destinations, over 7 million more people than Spain, in second place! It's not hard to see why, as France may have something to offer for everyone. Paris is known for it's art, culture, cuisine, fashion and romantic setting, and has several well-known landmarks, with the Eiffel Tower being the most visited paid monument in the world, with over 250 million visitors since it's construction. Outside Paris, the country has the very popular French Riviera (Cote D'Azur), France's coastline in the Mediterranean Sea and the French Alps, with western Europe's highest mountain, Mont Blanc.

## 41. NORTH KOREA IS HOME TO THE LARGEST FOOTBALL STADIUM IN THE WORLD.

In 1986, after the news that the Olympics was awarded to Seoul in South Korea, North Korea wanted to establish itself as the legitimate Korea, and hence created the Rungrado 1st Of May stadium, that was completed in time for the 1989 13th World Festival of Youth and Students, that saw 22,000 people compete. The stadium itself has a capacity of 114,000, 4,000 ahead of the second largest stadium, located in India and nearly 15,000 more than Europe's largest stadium, Camp Nou in Barcelona, Spain.

## 42. THE DEADLIEST ANIMALS IN AUSTRALIA AREN'T THE SNAKES OR SPIDERS.

In a report of animal related deaths in Australia between 2000 and 2010, there was a total of 254. 77 of these deaths were reported to be from horses, the majority of which caused from people falling off the horse. A further 33 came from cattle (trampling, car crashes) and 27 from dog attacks!

## 43. CHINA'S POPULATION TODAY IS MORE THAN EARTH'S POPULATION IN...

Today, China has a population of over 1.4 billion (1,400,000,000) people, over 4 times the population of the USA and 20 times the population of the UK. This was the Earth's population, just 150 years ago, in 1870! Attempts to curb China's huge population, include the One Child Policy, deemed at the time the most extreme example of population planning, and today, the more relaxed Two Child Policy. This indeed may have slowed China's population growth as India is set to be the world's most populous country in the near future!

## 44. IF THE WORLD'S POPULATION SQUEEZED TOGETHER AND STOOD SIDE BY SIDE, THEY COULD FIT INSIDE...

With some simple calculations and some assumptions, the 7.8 billion people when fully packed together, could fit in an area of 502.7 sq miles (1302 sq km), the total area of the city Los Angeles! This, of course, doesn't go to say that the world population could comfortably live in L.A.

## 45. THE OZONE LAYER THAT PROTECTS US FROM DEADLY RADIATION WILL MAKE A FULL RECOVERY.

In the second half of the 20th century, Freon was used in refrigerators and aerosols until scientists discovered that the stable molecules reached the ozone layer before decomposing, and therefore depleting the ozone. This was bad, as ozone protects Earth from most of the damaging radiation, so Freon and similar substances were soon internationally banned. Ozone holes appeared in places such as Antarctica, where large amounts of UV radiation was detected. Fortunately, the ozone in the ozone layer is constantly produced from oxygen, so in the absence of molecules with potential to interfere in this reaction (ozone depleting substances), then the ozone will replenish. This was confirmed in the 2000's, as monitoring of these 'Ozone Holes' indicated that areas of lower ozone levels were shrinking.

$$\boxed{O_3}$$

## 46. NEPAL'S FLAG IS SHAPED LIKE THE MOUNTAINS.

Nepal's flag is the only flag in the world that isn't rectangular. Infact, the flag is formed of two triangles, each a pennant to showcase the wonderful mountains within the country.

## 47. THERE'S ONLY 3 COUNTRIES IN THE WORLD THAT DON'T USE THE METRIC SYSTEM.

The metric system was first introduced in France in 1790s ,whilst the imperial system was a system introduced in the 1820s across the British Empire, so commonwealth countries also adopted the Imperial System. Gradually, the metric system replaced Imperial in most countries, except for Liberia, Myanmar and the United States - which is why each measurement of distance, weight and temperature in this book have bracketed measurements afterwards! These countries adopt imperial measures for everything such as volume (gallon, pint), weight (stone, pound, ounce), area (acres) and distance (inch, foot, yard, mile). Some countries hang on to some imperial measurements, for example, in the UK, road signs will display miles, and speedometers in mph. On the contrary, the U.S. has adopted some metric measures, such as gigabytes for a computer's memory.

## 48. THIS IS THE MOST POPULAR NAME IN THE WORLD.

The most popular name in the world is believed to be Muhammad. The name takes after the Islamic prophet and such naming comes from a religious tradition of naming the first-born son. As Islam has well over 1 billion followers, it is easy to see how this statistic came to be.

## 49. PURPLE IS ALMOST ABSENT FROM ALL COUNTRY FLAGS.

When you look at all the country flags, you start to get a feel of recurring sets of colors (blue, white, red, green, black etc.) but a few seem to just never come up, but for a fair reason. Purple is one of those colors, was used alot in royalty, and it was indeed a desirable and honorable color to have. Purple was, until the 1850s, a very expensive dye color to obtain, gram for gram more expensive than gold. For this reason, the only 2 flags with a splash of purple were designed after the 1850s, when synthetic purple dye was discovered. That is the reason why purple doesn't really show up, it wouldve been extremely expensive to blazon an army with a country flag containing purple, for example.

## 50. DO YOU LOVE PETS? HERE'S THE COUNTRY THAT LOVES THEM THE MOST TOO.

If you lived in New Zealand, you would, on average, have at least one pet in your house. 68% of homes in New Zealand have at least 1 pet in them. The United States is also a big fan, with estimates saying over half of all U.S. households own at least 1 pet.

# 51. YOU MAY KNOW SOMEONE RELATED TO MONGOL RULER, GENGHIS KHAN

Genghis Khan ruled over the second largest empire in history, only behind the British Empire. Whilst doing so, he fathered countless number of children, and while no exact number has been said, historians agree that there are alot, so much so infact, that 1 in 200 men in this world are estimated to be direct descendants of him! So, when you are out and about in town, count 200 men, and on average, 1 will be related to this 13th century ruler.

# 52. IN THIS COUNTRY, CERTAIN AREAS RAISE CHILDREN WITH DIFFERENT LANGUAGES THAN OTHER AREAS.

This country totals 4 official languages, French, German, Italian and Romansh. Furthermore, a large portion of people are able to speak English. If you haven't already guessed, this country is Switzerland. The northern part of the country, in places such as Zurich, uses German and children are bought up speaking German. If you are born in the west, in places such as Geneva, then your life will be very different, as French is the main spoken language. And in the south, in places such as Lugano, you will be bought up speaking Italian. Despite parts of the country speaking different languages, the Swiss people have a strong national identity, united under common values of democracy and federalism, as well as Alpine symbolism.

## 53. NAURU, A PACIFIC ISLAND NATION HAS NO OFFICIAL CAPITAL CITY.

Interestingly, if you search in any fact book or on any website, you'll see that Nauru's capital is listed as Yaren. This is officially incorrect, as the republic has not specified a capital city.A capital city is any municipality exercising primary control of an administrative region, usually including the seat of the government. Whilst Yaren is home to the houses of parliament (making Yaren a viable capital and therefore being listed as so), Yaren is a district of Nauru and is not the actual municipality.

## 54. ARE YOU A TALL PERSON? YOU'LL FIND MANY MORE LIKE YOU HERE.

If you are a tall person in your home country, it's likely that you may not stand out so much in The Netherlands, the country with the tallest average population in the world. People here average a height of 5 feet 8 inches (175cm), over an inches (2.5cm) more than in the United States, with Dutch males averaging 6 feet (183cm) and females averages 5 feet 6 inches (168cm). On the contrary, Indonesia is home to the world's shortest population, with people here averaging just 5 feet 2 inches (158cm)!

## 55. HERE'S THE 2 PLACES YOU WILL NOT BE ABLE TO GET COCA COLA®.

If you travel to a less touristy destination, say a country in Africa or Central Asia, you may be comforted when you see brands you recognise, such as McDonalds®, and Coca Cola®. However, there are 2 places that Coca Cola® is not officially found, because of long lasting U.S. trade embargos. These places are North Korea and Cuba. What this means is that the company's data state that the countries of Cuba and North Korea receive none from the U.S., but in practice, you may be able to still find it (at higher prices) as it may be imported from other countries.

## 56. MT. EVEREST'S SUMMIT ISN'T THE CLOSEST LAND TO SPACE.

At 8848 metres (29,049 feet), Mt. Everest is the tallest mountain on Earth, so this should also equate to it being the closest to space. However, the Earth is not perfectly spherical, the equatorial region of Earth 'bulges'. As a result of this, Ecuador's highest mountain, Mt Chimborazo, that stands at 6,263 metres (20,548 feet) actually reaches closer to space as it lies almost directly on the equator. Mt. Everest, located on the Nepalese – Chinese border, sits around 28 degrees north of the equator, a latitude found in Florida and southern Texas.

# 57. ON THE TOPIC OF MT. EVEREST, IT ISN'T ACTUALLY THE TALLEST MOUNTAIN IF YOU MEASURE IT THIS WAY...

Now this one is more of a technicality, but, if you measure the height of every mountain, from the base to summit, but measuring from it's underwater base, rather than sea level as the base, then you will find the Mauna Kea in Hawaii, measuring 4207 metres (13,803 feet), is the highest mountain in the world. From it's underwater base, Mauna Kea would measure 10,200 metres (33,500 feet), trumping Everest's 8848m (29,029ft).

# 58. CHINA, A COUNTRY LARGER THAN THE CONTIGUOUS UNITED STATES, HAS ONE TIME ZONE.

So, when its 7am in China's capital, Beijing, it is also 7am over 3000 miles (5000km) west in Urumqi. China spans 5 geographical time zones, but since the Communist Party of China's takeover in 1949, the whole country (officially) follows Beijing Time (UTC+8:00). The implications of this can be felt in the west of the country, if 7am in Beijing is when it gets light, the west of the country will remain dark until 9am. In Urumqi, people adopt to this with shifted working hours, with 10am to 7pm being commonplace, as is with shop opening hours. Urumqi, and the region of Xinjiang, also follow the Xinjiang time (UTC+6:00), 2 hours behind Beijing Time to make things a little more normal.

## 59. LOS ANGELES IS A SHORTENED VERSION OF THE ORIGINAL NAME OF THE CITY.

Los Angeles today is known globally as the home of Hollywood, and as a thriving metropolis popularised in media, film and gaming. However, as with every city, it began it's life as a small place, settled by 44 pueblos, who called the settlement - El Pueblo de Nuestra Señora la Reina de Los Ángeles. This translates to The Town of Our Lady the Queen of the Angels. The city through it's change of rule from Spanish, to Mexican, to American, retained the last part - 'Los Angeles' - of the original name, meaning The Angels.

## 60. AUSTRALIA IS WIDER THAN THE MOON.

Earth's moon is roughly 3470km (2200 miles) in diameter, which is actually less than the distance between the westernmost and easternmost points of Australia, which is nearly 4000km (2500 miles)!

## 61. WHILST IT SEEMS LIKE IT ALWAYS RAINS THERE, LONDON ISN'T ALL THAT WET.

London, and in fact the whole of the United Kingdom has gained a reputation for having a number of grey, rainy days. London receives around 109 days (slightly less than a third of the year) where over 1mm (0.04 inch) of rain is recorded. And whilst this is lot, the total annual rainfall in London is less than most other cities in the world, including Paris, Rome, New York, Shanghai, Tokyo, Singapore, Rio De Janeiro, Sydney and many more. The reputation therefore comes from a combination of rainy days (a good portion of it as drizzle) and low sunshine (London is more cloudy and sees less sunshine than the cities listed).

## 62. LONDON, BERLIN AND AMSTERDAM ARE ALL THE SAME LATITUDE AS SIBERIA.

This fun fact could have been worded in lots of different examples, all of which to convey just how northerly European cities are compared to those in other continents. Siberia is a huge geographical region in Russia, loosely associated with North Russia and is known for its extremely cold winters, nomadic population, and labor camps. Geographical Siberia actually encompasses most of Asian Russia and astonishingly, it's southernmost point in the Altai Republic is closer to the equator than the European cities of London, Berlin and Amsterdam!

# 63. WHAT IS THE DIFFERENCE BETWEEN A RAINFOREST AND A JUNGLE?

Through most of our childhood, the terms seem to be used interchangeably, referring to a tropical forest. Both terms can refer to a tropical forest, but with a few key differences! A rainforest is a forest with a thick tree canopy layer that blocks most of the sunlight from reaching the ground, and therefore restricting growth of plants on the forest floor. If this canopy thins, then a jungle forms as sunlight reaches the floor, and undergrowth forms as shrubs, vines and small trees. Whilst both are normally associated with tropical climates, both terms are not exclusive to it, and a rainforest in the tropics can be more specifically called a tropical rainforest, to differentitate it from a rainforest found in other biomes, such as temperate rainforests.

# 64. RAINFORESTS COVER AROUND 3% OF EARTH'S TOTAL AREA, BUT...

Rainforests are said to be home to around half of all species in the world. Estimates vary on the actual figure but most state that this is over 50% of all species. The Amazon rainforest circulates (not produces) about 20% of the world's oxygen. Rainforests are home to over quarter of all the natural medicines found, that go on to treat diseases such and cancer.

## 65. THIS GUARDED WALL DIVIDED THIS EUROPEAN CITY FOR 28 YEARS.

Completed in 1961, the intentions with this monument weren't so bright. At the time, Germany was split into 2, and communist East Germany faced a crisis with a good portion of it's population immigrating into West Germany, so a guarded wall was erected, circling the whole of West Berlin and effectively splitting the city in 2. The official reason for the wall was to prevent fascist (western) elements from conspiring to dismantle an East German socialist state. Containing mines, death strips, guard towers, soldiers with shoot-to-kill orders and electrified fences, the wall claimed many lives of defectors, until it's fall in 1989, and today, is one of the most notorious reminders of the world's Cold War era.

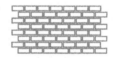

## 66. THIS IS THE CLOSEST U.S. STATE TO MAINLAND AFRICA.

When calculating the distance between places and taking into account the curvature of the Earth, the U.S. state of Maine comes closest to Africa! Considering the locations of Africa and the USA on the map, it may seem like Florida is closest to Africa, but Lubec, Maine takes this title! It is 3150 miles (5070km) from El Beddouza, Morocco.

# 67. ASIA IS HOME TO MORE PEOPLE THAN EVERY OTHER CONTINENT COMBINED.

Asia, with around 4.6 billion people as of 2020, is not only the most populous continent, it is more populous than the 6 other continents COMBINED! Infact, if China or India were continents, they would be the 2nd most populous continents in the world, ahead of the whole of Africa!

# 68. THE STATUE OF LIBERTY WAS ORIGINALLY A TOTALLY DIFFERENT COLOR.

The Statue Of Liberty is a massive sculpture and a symbol of New York. It was gifted from the people of France to the people of the United States. Originally designed by Bartholdi and built by Gustave Eifel (the same person who built the Eiffel Tower) the Statue of Liberty was completed and dedicated in 1886. The statue is made of Copper, so when it was originally completed, the color of the statue was Copper orange. Over time, the Copper of the statue oxidised in Earth's atmosphere (similar to Iron and rust), and the statue turned into the turquoise color you see today.

# 69. AROUND 90% OF THE WORLD'S POPULATION LIVES NORTH OF THE EQUATOR.

The northern hemisphere contains 67.3% of Earth's land mass, but 90% of the world's population! This imbalance can be easily explained by the largely inhospitable southern hemisphere, notably the Australian Desert and Antartica. The remaining hospitable areas in Oceania, South America and Africa is a lot less than the hospitable areas in the northern hemisphere. Furthermore, Christmas in the Southern Hemisphere is celebrated during the summer! Something that takes a bit of getting used to if you are from the northern hemisphere.

# 70. AFRICA'S MOST SPOKEN LANGUAGE IS ARABIC.

Between the 1.3 billion people that live in Africa, over 2000 native languages are spoken. The effects of colonisation in Africa's history is reflected in the most widely spoken languages, with around 170 million people speaking Arabic, 130 million speaking English, 115 million speaking French, and 100 million speaking Swahili, the largest native African language by number of speakers!

# 71. MT. EVEREST AND THE HIMALAYA MOUNTAIN RANGE IS GROWING.

By nearly an inch (2.5cm) a year! The mountains were born when the Indian tectonic plate crashed into the Eurasian tectonic plate, roughly 55 million years ago. The collision of the two plates result in the rise of mountains in the collision zone, and because they are still colliding into each other today, the mountains are continuing to grow.

# 72. THE SERENGETI IS HOME TO ONE OF THE WORLD'S LARGEST ANIMAL MIGRATIONS.

The Serengeti is a National Park in the north of Tanzania, in Africa, and maybe one of the most well-known spots for going on an animal Safari. Safari literally translating to 'Journey' in Swahili, in reference to the great migration seeing millions of animals pass through every year. The estimates suggest that around 1.7 million wildebeest, 470,000 gazelles and 260,000 zebras. Above this, the Serengeti is known as a habitat for a large amount of predators, such as Lions, Tigers, Hyenas and Leopards.

# 73. THERE IS A SEA THAT HAS NO COASTLINE.

The Sargasso Sea is found in the Atlantic Ocean, close to Bermuda, and is the only sea in the world without a coastline (land boundaries). The border of the sea is formed from the four ocean gyres that surround it. Unlike the majority of the rest of the Atlantic Ocean, the water here is calm, and therefore seaweed often covers the waters, the name of the seaweed, Sargassum, being the namesake of the sea.

# 74. THE GREAT PYRAMID OF GIZA IS WEIRDER THAN YOU THINK.

The Great Pyramids of Giza is a massive feat of engineering in today's world, let alone for a civilization that existed 5000 years ago. The pyramid initially stood at 146 metres (479 feet), formed of 2.3 million blocks weighing a total of 6 million tons, and was thought to be constructed in 20 years. Today's estimates suggest that 20,000 people was needed to accomplish such a task. The attention of detail is impressive, with intricate details like the near perfect angles of the pyramid and the maze of a tunnelling system, inferring the use of some sort of technology. Blocks weighing up to 15 tons were lifted up to 140 metres (459 feet) and then placed perfectly, and the pyramid lies very close to the true north-south, aligning with celestial bodies. The list of mysteries continues...

## 75. IF YOU ARE A FAN OF CAVES, YOU WILL LOVE THIS PLACE!

For some people, claustrophobia sets in when you enter a cave, your phone signal disappears and you start thinking about what would happen if the electricity keeping the lights on in the cave shuts off. For others, caves are a playground, and if this is you, then the U.S. state of Kentucky is the place for you! The Mammoth Cave National Park has the longest cave system in the world, boasting over 400 miles (640 km) of surveyed passageways, and possibly many more miles that are yet to be explored. Furthermore, these caves are the only place you may find the endangered Kentucky Cave Shrimp, a sightless, albino shrimp.

## 76. IF YOU ARE LOOKING FOR THE LONGEST COMMERCIAL FLIGHT IN THE WORLD, HEAD OVER TO NEW JERSEY.

Taking over 18 hours and covering over 9500 miles (15,288km), the direct flight from Newark, New Jersey in the USA to Singapore (in Singapore, the country) is the longest commercial flight you can take in 2020. Plans for direct flights from New York to Sydney would topple this record, with a distance of over 9900 miles (15,932km).

## 77. THE ANGKOR WAT IS THE LARGEST RELIGIOUS BUILDING IN THE WORLD.

The Angkor Wat, a remarkable piece of architecture found in Cambodia, is a buddhist temple measuring 1.6 square km (402 acres) in size. If it were a country, it wouldn't even be the smallest (Vatican city would be). The Angkor Wat was constructed by the Khmer King, Suryavarman II, in the 12th century as a Hindu Temple, but around the 13th century, the complex was gradually transformed into a Buddhist place of worship. The temple complex today is a synonymous with Cambodian culture, and as such, it is found on the Cambodian flag.

## 78. SUDAN HAS MORE ANCIENT PYRAMIDS THAN EGYPT.

Despite the fame of the well-known great pyramids of Giza in Egypt, the country doesn't hold the title for the most amount of pyramids. Egypt has a total of 138 and Sudan, a country directly south of Egypt, has an even more impressive 250 pyramids! Most of these were built for the Kushite kingdoms of Nubia.

## 79. DON'T LOOK DOWN! HERE'S THE TALLEST BRIDGE IN THE WORLD.

If you head to the Chinese provinces of Guizhou and Yunnan, you may find the Duge Bridge, a bridge spanning 1,340 m (4,400 ft) and sitting over a whopping 565 metres (1,850 feet) the Beipan river below. For perspective, the tallest building in New York City could fit underneath this bridge upright. The bridge was completed in 2016 to shorten the drive time between the Chinese cities of Xuanwei city, Yunnan and Shuicheng County, Guizhou.

## 80. NEW YORK'S 'BIG APPLE' NICKNAME CAME FROM A HORSE RACE PRIZE.

In the 1920's, New York would come to take up the nickname from a horse racing column in the newspaper that would start it's writing with winning the "big apple" in New York. Originally referring to the large prize money at the end of the race, bettors that would win the prize came back, refering to the city as the "big apple" on account of the wins. The term caught on within the horse racing community, and by the 1930's, its usage spread outside of horse racing, and began seeing use in music, theater and by the general population.

## 81. THIS CAPITAL CITY MAY LEAVE YOU MORE BREATHLESS THAN NORMAL.

If you head to Bolivia's capital city, La Paz, you may feel a little breathless down to it's altitude. The majority of the city sits at around 3600 metres (11,811 feet), making it the highest altitude city in the world, with parts of the city even reaching above 4000 metres (13,000 feet). At this altitude, if you try and do your morning jog, a session at the gym or other exercise, you will feel a shortness of breath, as the oxygen is thinner here. At these altitudes, you will also need your coat year round, as average temperatures during the year range from 13°C (55.4°F) to 17°C (62.6°F), and frost in the mornings are common, whichever month you go.

## 82. SWEDEN IS HOME TO OVER 267,000 ISLANDS.

Sweden has the most islands of any country, beating the island nations of Indonesia and the Philippines, with around 17,000 and 7167 islands respectively. The average size of the islands found in Sweden are much lower however, with all 267,000 islands totalling just 3% of Sweden's land area, or around 12,000 sq km (4633 sq mi). Therefore, on average, each island is only 0.05 sq km (0.019 sq mi), or around 8 football pitches worth.

## 83. JAMAICA'S COUNTRY FLAG IS THE ONLY ONE IN THE WORLD THAT DOESN'T CONTAIN, BLUE, WHITE OR RED.

Jamaica's flag colors consist of black, green and yellow, and was adopted on Jamaica's independence day in 1962. The color yellow represents the sun, the color green representing the land and black represents the hardships the country underwent. Mauritania qualified in this list, until 2017, when they added 2 red stripes to their green and gold flag design.

## 84. PENGUINS ARE NOT JUST FOUND IN ANTARCTICA.

Penguins are not just found in Antarctica, and we are not talking about those found in zoos either. Contrary to their depiction, especially in film, they can be found native in South America, Oceania, Australia and even Africa. While being almost entirely in the Southern Hemisphere, they may be found on Ecuador's Galapagos Islands, some of which are just north of the equator. The largest and arguably the most iconic penguin (depicted below), known as the Emperor penguin, is endemic (native) to Antarctica however.

## 85. BETWEEN 1939 AND 2020, SOME 130 NEW COUNTRIES HAVE FORMED.

In 1939, there was only 65 countries in the world. The rise in number of countries is due to the effects of World War 2 and it's aftermath, the subsequent decolonisation of the world during the cold war, especially in the 1960s and 1970s, the break-up of the Soviet Union and Yugoslavia and the formation of many Pacific Island nations. The decolonisation of the British and French empires alone contributed to the creation of over 50 new countries!

## 86. TAMPICO, MEXICO IS ONE OF THE FEW COASTAL TROPICAL PLACES THAT HAS SEEN SNOWFALL.

Tampico sits on the Gulf of Mexico in the Mexican state of Tamaulipas. The town has a plentiful array of palm trees and balmy weather all year round, however, as with most of the USA's deep south, temperatures here can drop to unusually low temperatures, and February 4, 1895, the town experienced a snowfall. Snowfalls in the tropics are extremely rare, as the definition for a tropical place is  and this snowfall may set the North American for the furthest south recorded snowfall at a coastal location.

## 87. THE MEDITERRANEAN SEA IS 8 MILES (13KM) AWAY FROM BEING A LAKE.

The distance mentioned is the distance between the Southern extreme of mainland Spain and the northern extreme of Morocco. This distance, less than a third of the distance of the English channel, is what connects the Mediterranean Sea to the rest of the Atlantic Ocean. History suggests that if the gap were to close, the Mediterranean Sea would not be a lake for long, as an event some 5.5 million years ago, saw the gap close and soon resulted in the Mediterranean Sea drying up, known as the Messinian Salinity crisis. If this were to occur today, it would be disastrous for European countries with coastlines on the Mediterranean, as rainfall would stop, and the once green nations would likely turn into desert. Thankfully, the Mediterranean filled up after the Zanclean flood, where the Atlantic Ocean reclaimed the Mediterranean.

## 88. AFRICA IS THE ONLY CONTINENT TO BE SITUATED IN ALL 4 HEMISPHERES

Earth is dissected into 4 hemispheres using the Equator to define the northern and southern hemispheres, and the Prime Meridian to define the western and eastern hemispheres. As Africa is the only continent that both the prime meridian and equator crosses, it therefore is the only one in all 4 hemispheres.

# 89. GREENLAND IS ALOT SMALLER THAN YOU MAY THINK.

In certain projections for the world that you may have seen, specifically the Mercator projection that is used in most mapping systems today because it preserves the angles of the latitudes and longitudes of the globe, making it a conformal (and therefore mathematically accurate) projection. A side-effect of this projection is that inflation of land accelerates towards the poles. This feature affects the whole world and not just Greenland, but Greenland is a great benchmark example of just how elongated the Mercator projection is. Next time you go on the internet, click maps and zoom out. In reality, Greenland (with an area of 2,166,086 sq km; 836,330 sq miles) should be slightly larger than Mexico (with an area of 1,972,550 sq km; 761,610 sq miles). But what you will see, is Mexico could fit in Greenland many times over... such as in the Mercator Projection below.

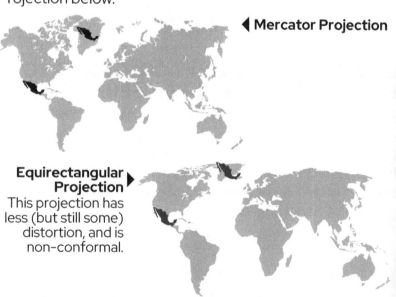

◀ **Mercator Projection**

**Equirectangular ▶ Projection**
This projection has less (but still some) distortion, and is non-conformal.

## 90. IF YOU HAVE 8 DAYS SPARE, THEN THE TRANS-SIBERIAN HIGHWAY CAN OFFER A NICE GETAWAY.

Connecting the west and east of Russia and spanning 8 time zones, this railway route takes you through the heart of Russia, where you will see just about all that the country is made of. Not only that, if you travel along this 9,289 km (5,772 mile) route, you will also cross a record breaking 3901 bridges! Since being in operation in 1916, the railway principally connects Moscow with Vladivostok.

## 91. THE EXTINCT DODO BIRD WAS ONCE NATIVE TO THIS ISLAND NATION.

The Dodo bird happened to be one of the best examples to this day of an extinction of an animal species caused by human activity. Dodo was a flightless bird that was endemic (native) to the island nation of Mauritius, east of Madagascar. It was believed to be first sighted in the 1590s by Dutch sailors. A combination of them being hunted by sailors and invasive species (non-native species introduced into the environment) as well as destruction of their habitat, led to the Dodo becoming extinct in 1662. The extinction of the Dodo was one of the first examples of a human influenced extinction, and was popularized by the story of Alice's Adventures in Wonderland.

## 92. SAN FRANCISCO'S SUMMER IS COLDER THAN MOST OF SIBERIA'S SUMMER.

If you head to downtown San Francisco during the summer, coming in from adjacent areas such as San Jose, then you may feel a sharp drop in temperature, and that the light clothes are not enough to keep you warm. Downtown San Francisco has a very mild mediterranean climate with little seasonal variation, caused by the cool currents of the Pacific Ocean, and the surrounding moderating effect of San Francisco bay. What results, is a brisk wind that can occur for most of the year, and astonishingly mild summer temperatures for it's latitude (around the same as South Spain), which at it's highest in September is just 21.2°C (70.2°F). This is the coolest of any major American city, and even cooler than some of the largest cities in Siberia, such as Yakutsk, whose summer high temperatures are a warm 25.5°C (77.9°F). This situation is not unique, as South American cities that lie on the Pacific Ocean, such as Lima, Peru, have very dry and mild climates because of the effect of cool ocean currents. Other places that are affected include West Africa and the Canary Islands, South West Africa and Western Australia.

## 93. ILLINOIS IN THE UNITED STATES WAS HOME TO THE WORLD'S TALLEST PERSON.

Robert Wadlow, known as the Giant of Illinois, was born in 1918 in Alton, Illinois and went on to grow to a mind blowing height of 8 ft 11.1 in (2.72 m) at the time of his death. He was not abnormal in birth, weighing and measuring as an average newborn, but within a few months, Robert grew abnormally fast, attributed to high levels of Human Growth Hormone. At 7 years of age, Robert was the same height as an average adult male, at 9 years of age, it was reported that he was strong enough to carry his father up a flight of stairs, and at 17 years of age, at 8 ft 3 in (2.51 m), his height matched the height of the tallest living person today, Sultan Kösen. He died at age 22 from an infection, where his tallest height was recorded.

## 94. THERE ARE 3 COUNTRIES THAT ARE COMPLETELY SURROUNDED BY ANOTHER COUNTRY.

These 3 countries are San Marino, Vatican City and Lesotho. This is a separate definition to countries that are bordered by only 1 other country ,which by definition will include these 3 countries, but also countries such as Canada. San Marino and Vatican City are both completely surrounded by Italy, and Lesotho is surrounded by South Africa.

## 95. AROUND 75% OF ALL TORNADOS OCCUR IN THE UNITED STATES

Tornado expert Tom Grazulis estimates that around 75% of all tornadoes that occur in a given year will be located in the United States. This in practice means that the U.S. will receive around 1000 tornadoes a year, mostly in the Tornado Alley, that stretches from Texas to South Dakota. On a yearly basis, Texas will receive the most tornadoes of any state, averaging well over 100 in a year! The winds of these tornadoes can travel up to 300mph (482 km/h), and destruction paths can be as long as 50 miles (80km) and 1 mile wide (1.6km). However, most of the tornadoes last less than 10 minutes, and most will see wind speeds of less than 110 mph (180 km/h), the border of F1 (moderate damage) and F2 (considerable damage) on the Fujita Scale that ranks tornadoes from F0 to F5 by damage caused.

## 96. THE WORLD'S LARGEST ROCK IN AUSTRALIA IS NOT WHAT YOU THINK.

By know, you will be familiar with Uluru /Ayer's Rock, but that isn't the answer to this one. Infact, another rock in Australia called Mount Augustus, which despite the name, is not a mountain but instead a rock that sits over 700 metres (2300 feet) and can be seen from 100 miles away. It is therefore double the size of Uluru!

# 97. THE USA TRIED TO PURCHASE GREENLAND ON SEVERAL OCCASIONS.

Greenland, the largest island in the world, sits geographically in the North American arctic, but politically and historically a European island and territory of Denmark. The USA purchased land from Russia (Alaska), France (French Louisiana), Mexico (Gadsden Purchase) and even from Denmark (Danish West Indies), but an offer was never accepted for the sale of Greenland. Following the United States' Alaska purchase in 1867 was the first time the States considered the acquisition of Greenland. The president considered annexation however, in a similar way to their annexation of the Kingdom of Hawaii. This never happened, and the U.S.A's next serious proposal came in 1946, when the United States offered Denmark $100 million in gold bullion for Greenland. Despite the island being almost occupied by U.S. military personnel, due to its strategic location in the Cold War, Denmark refused the offer and expected the Americans to leave the island. U.S. presence persisted, and in 1951, Denmark officially acknowledged via a treaty that the U.S. would have control of aspects of the island, for as long as the NATO treaty existed. In 2019, President Trump discussed the purchase of Greenland off Denmark, but the Danish Prime Minister quickly rejected the idea. Today, if Greenland was successfully purchased from Denmark, the United States would easily be the second largest country in the world, and it would be the USA's largest acquisition to date. However, just over 50,000 people live on Greenland, so the United States' population would not increase by much.

## 98. IF YOU DO NOT LIKE THE RAIN, THEN IT'S BEST YOU AVOID MAWSYNRAM.

Mawsynram, located in Meghalaya, India, holds the official record for the wettest place on Earth. The town receives 11,872 millimetres (467.4 inches) of rainfall annually. For comparison, if you live in a house, this rainfall amount will most likely be taller than your house. If it fell as snow in one go, it would equate to over 100 metres (110 yards) of snowfall. For comparison to other cities, Monrovia in Liberia is regarded as the wettest capital in the world, with an annual rainfall of 4624mm (181 inches).

## 99. JUST HOW LONG IS THE GREAT WALL OF CHINA?

Various portions of The Great Wall of China's construction started as early as 700BC, built to protect the ancient Chinese states from various Eurasian nomadic groups, although later, uses included taxation of goods passing through the Silk Road. The most well-known sections were built during the Ming dynasty between 1368 and 1644, and attract around 50 million visitors every year. Estimates state that the Great Wall section by the Ming Dynasty totalled around 8,850 km (5,500 miles), with 6,259 km (3,889 miles) of actual wall (as oppose to natural blockades such as rivers and mountains). The total length of all the walls, including the branches, was 21,196 km (13,171 miles) - which works out to around half the distance of the equator!

## 100. IT'S DIFFICULT FOR RUSSIA TO SH GOODS OVERSEAS.

Russia, the largest country in the world, has always experienced difficulties when shipping goods overseas. reason for this is both a geographical and political one. Suppose Russia wanted to ship goods to Cuba in the winter In east and north Russia, this is not possible as the sea around all its ports in the winter are generally frozen over. In west Russia, the country borders the Baltic Sea, however, Russia would need to pass the territorial waters of Denmark or Germany in order to reach Cuba. Russia is connected to the Black sea, but again, it would need to pass the territorial waters of Turkey to reach Cuba. This issue was particularly prominent in the Cold War, as Denmark, (west) Germany and Turkey were all NATO (U.S. aligned) countries.

## 101. ABOUT OF THIRD OF EARTH'S LAND AREA IS DESERT.

That's right, desert is the most common biome found on land, and experts predict that this percentage will increase as global warming is leading to climate change. Major areas of desert include the Sahara Desert, Sonora Desert, Arabian Desert, Antarctica, Patagonian Desert and the Gobi Desert. For the time being, the second most is forest, claiming a further 30% of Earth's land.

## - THE AMAZON RAINFOREST ꓳODUCE 20% OF THE WORLD'S

ᴢon rainforest is mistakenly labelled the lungs of ⱨth by various media outlets, who go on to claim that ᴀmazon rainforest produces 20% of the world's ⱪygen. This is essentially impossible, because tree's produce oxygen via photosynthesis, a reaction that consumes carbon dioxide and water to produce glucose and oxygen. One molecule of carbon dioxide therefore produces one molecule of oxygen, according to the reaction below, which essentially makes the original claim defunct, as only 0.04% Earth's atmosphere is Carbon Dioxide. As photosynthesis uses six molecules of carbon dioxide to create six molecules of oxygen, the study of stoichiometry indicates that the rainforest in the Amazon is able to generate a maximum of 0.04% of Earth's Oxygen's supply (at any one time). Around 21% of the atmosphere contains Oxygen, so there is just not enough Carbon Dioxide for this fact to the true. Estimates to the Amazon rainforest's total contribution to Earth's Oxygen range from 6-9% according to scientists, but that's not all, as another process within the tree called cellular respiration takes in Oxygen, in a reverse reaction to photosynthesis, and it thought that the two reactions basically cancel out and leave the Amazon rainforest a zero net contributor to Earth's Oxygen supply.

$$6CO_2 + 6H_2O \rightarrow C_6H_{12}O_6 + 6O_2$$

*Photosynthesis reaction*

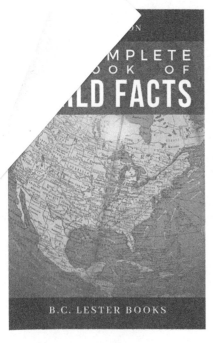

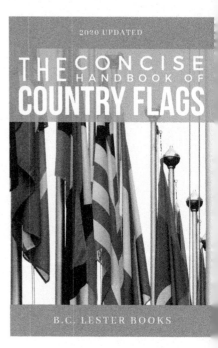